KLONDIKE TRIES TO TOUCH THE CHILDREN.

TIME FOR A NAP.

BIG BROTHERS PLAY ROUGH SOMETIMES.

"LET'S WALK TOGETHER."

"LEFT, RIGHT, LEFT, RIGHT. . ."

POLAR BEAR MATH

LEARNING ABOUT FRACTIONS
FROM KLONDIKE AND SNOW

BY ANN WHITEHEAD NAGDA
AND CINDY BICKEL

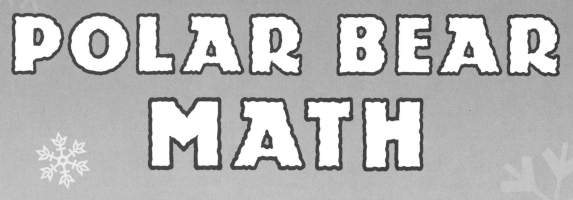

Henry Holt and Company

New York

Thanks to Roberta Flexer, Lisa Mesple, Phyllis Perry, Candy Hyde, Marcy Lockhart, Judy Minger, Linda Erickson, Fran Jenner, Shelley Fitzgerald, Penny Altberg, Kirit Nagda, and Reka Simonsen, my patient and supportive editor, for helping with the math

To Cindy Bickel, Dave Kenny, Angela Baier, Clayton Freiheit, and all the other wonderful people who work and volunteer at the Denver Zoo
—A. W. N.

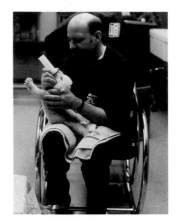

I would like to dedicate this book to the memory of Denver Zoo veterinary technician Denny Roling, my friend and colleague, who loved all the zoo animals and was especially fond of Klondike and Snow.
—C. B.

DENNY WITH KLONDIKE, HIS FAVORITE BEAR.

Henry Holt and Company, LLC, *Publishers since 1866*
115 West 18th Street, New York, New York 10011
www.henryholt.com

Henry Holt is a registered trademark of Henry Holt and Company, LLC
Text and story concept copyright © 2004 by Ann Whitehead Nagda
Photographs copyright © 2004 by the Denver Zoological Foundation, Inc.
All rights reserved. Distributed in Canada by H. B. Fenn and Company Ltd.

Photo credits: All images by Cindy Bickel with the following exceptions:
Dave Kenny: cover, 15, 17, 30 (top), 31 (both); Ann Nagda: 2 (bottom), 6, 8, 9, 19, 21;
John Edwards: 3 (bottom left), 5, 7, 13, 18, 28; Steve Bickel: 20; Marian Edwards: 29; Kathy Ogsbury: 30 (bottom).

Library of Congress Cataloging-in-Publication Data
Nagda, Ann Whitehead
Polar bear math : learning about fractions from Klondike and Snow / by Ann Whitehead Nagda and Cindy Bickel.
p.   cm.
Summary: Uses charts and recipes for bear milk prepared for two baby polar bears born in a zoo to teach about fractions.
1. Fractions—Juvenile literature. [1. Fractions. 2. Polar bear. 3. Bears. 4. Animals—Infancy.] I. Bickel, Cindy. II. Title.
QA117.N24 2004   513.2'6—dc22   2003020996

ISBN 0-8050-7301-9 / EAN 978-0-8050-7301-0
First Edition—2004 / Designed by Christy Hale
Printed in the United States of America on acid-free paper. ∞

1 3 5 7 9 10 8 6 4 2

A NEWBORN BEAR IS JUST A HANDFUL.

INTRODUCTION

Most people never see newborn polar bear cubs, because they stay in a den with their mother until they are three or four months old. But when a polar bear mother at the Denver Zoo abandoned her cubs, the public got to witness their struggle to survive from the day they were born. This book uses charts and recipes for bear milk to help tell the story of Klondike and Snow, two polar bears who were hand-raised at the Denver Zoo. If you want to read the story of the bear cubs without the math, you can read only the right-hand pages of this book. Then to learn more and see how fractions were used while raising the bears, you can look at the left-hand pages as well.

MOTHER POLAR BEARS

A **fraction** is a part of a whole or a part of a group, or set. Here is a set of animals: three mother bears. Each mother bear is one part, or one fraction, of the set.

3 MOTHER BEARS

The total number of equal parts in a set is always on the bottom of the fraction and is called the **denominator**. The number of parts you are dealing with is always on the top of the fraction and is called the **numerator.**

On average, two out of every three mother polar bears have twin babies. We can show this with the fraction below. In this fraction the denominator is 3, because there are three bears in the set, and the numerator is 2, because two of the bears in this set have twins.

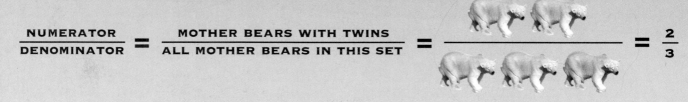

$$\frac{\text{NUMERATOR}}{\text{DENOMINATOR}} = \frac{\text{MOTHER BEARS WITH TWINS}}{\text{ALL MOTHER BEARS IN THIS SET}} = \frac{2}{3}$$

Of the three mother bears, one does not have twins. We can show this with the fraction below. In this fraction the denominator is still 3, but the numerator is 1, because one bear does not have twins.

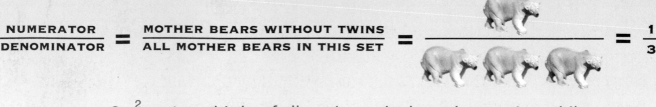

$$\frac{\text{NUMERATOR}}{\text{DENOMINATOR}} = \frac{\text{MOTHER BEARS WITHOUT TWINS}}{\text{ALL MOTHER BEARS IN THIS SET}} = \frac{1}{3}$$

So $\frac{2}{3}$, or two-thirds, of all mother polar bears have twins, while $\frac{1}{3}$, or one-third, of all mother bears do not have twins.

ULU, LIKE TWO-THIRDS OF ALL POLAR BEAR
MOTHERS, HAD TWIN BEAR CUBS.

Early one November morning at the Denver Zoo, a polar bear named Ulu gave birth to two baby bears. She cleaned them off, then left them lying on the cold cement floor of the hallway that led to her den. When Gary, the polar bear keeper, came to work, he heard soft crying. Gary could see that Ulu was in her den, but there were two small shapes in the hallway. When he looked closer, he found the newborn polar bear twins that Ulu had abandoned. Gary tucked the babies inside his jacket and rushed them to the zoo hospital.

COMMON DENOMINATORS

Fractions that have the same denominators are said to have **common denominators**. It is easy to add fractions if they have common denominators—you can simply add the numerators (the denominator does not change). In the example below, the two fractions from page 8 are added together.

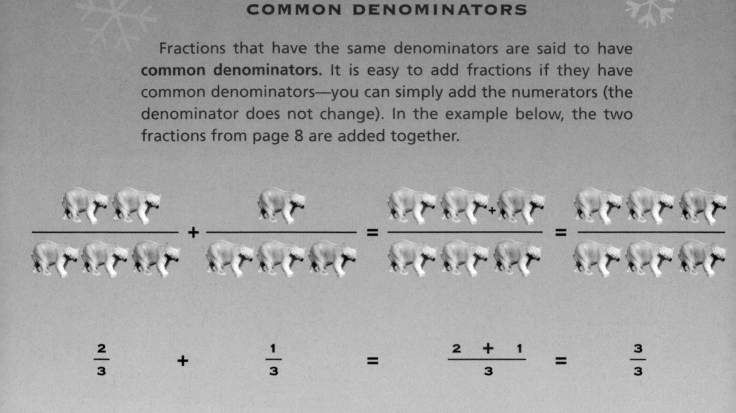

$$\frac{2}{3} \quad + \quad \frac{1}{3} \quad = \quad \frac{2 + 1}{3} \quad = \quad \frac{3}{3}$$

In the resulting fraction, both the numerator and the denominator are 3. When the numerator and the denominator are the same, a fraction is equal to 1, or one whole set.

 = **1 SET OF MOTHER BEARS**

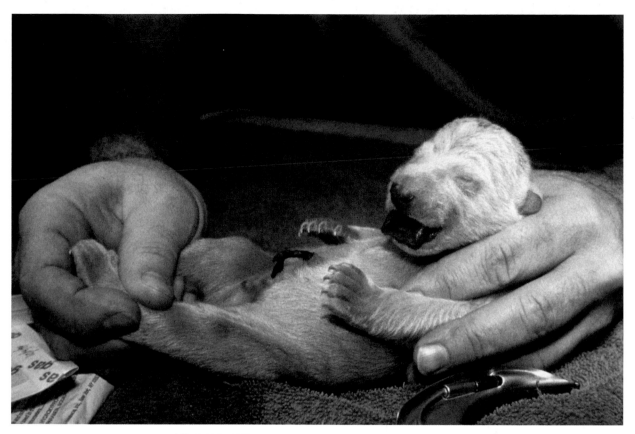

KLONDIKE IS ONLY A FEW HOURS OLD.

Dr. Kenny, the zoo veterinarian, examined the cubs. They had fine white hair covering their pink skin, and their eyes were closed. They weighed slightly over one pound each, a typical weight for newborn polar bears. Gary, the keeper, named the male cub Klondike and the female cub Snow. Klondike had a cut on his head, possibly caused by Ulu picking him up in her mouth to move him. Both cubs were frail and very cold. Dr. Kenny didn't think they would live.

However, he asked Cindy, a veterinary technician, to take care of the bears, because she had raised many baby animals. The bears were put in a human infant incubator to raise their body temperatures. Several hours later, when Klondike had warmed up, Dr. Kenny stitched the cut on his head.

11

MAKING POLAR BEAR MILK

Cindy used a recipe to make polar bear milk. She mixed 1 cup of puppy milk with 2 cups of half-and-half to create a whole amount of 3 cups.

PUPPY MILK   **HALF-AND-HALF**

Since the whole amount was in three equal parts, you could say:

One part, or $\frac{1}{3}$, was puppy milk.
Two parts, or $\frac{2}{3}$, were half-and-half.

After the milk was mixed, cod-liver oil and vitamins were added.

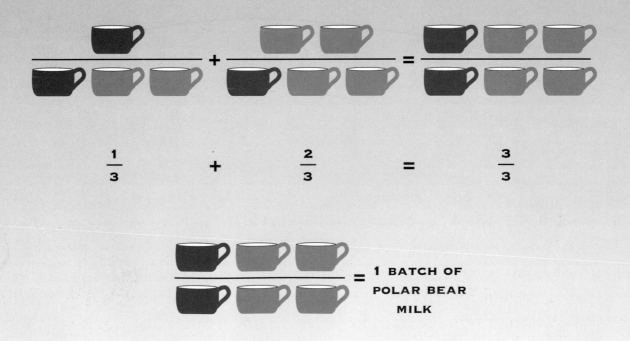

$$\frac{1}{3} \quad + \quad \frac{2}{3} \quad = \quad \frac{3}{3}$$

= **1 BATCH OF POLAR BEAR MILK**

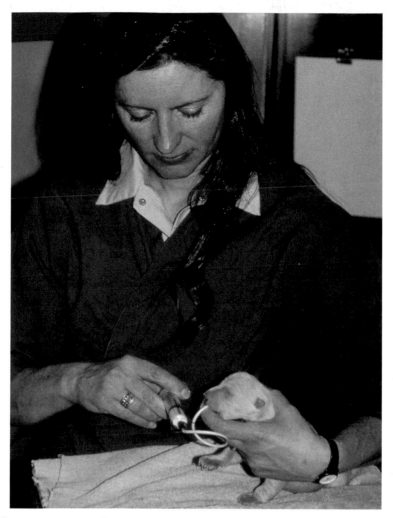

CINDY GIVES SNOW MILK THROUGH A FEEDING TUBE.

Because the cubs were very weak, Cindy fed them sugar water at first. Soon they would need milk. But what formula would be just right for polar bear cubs? Cindy did some research and learned that polar bear milk looks like heavy cream, smells fishy, and is high in fat. When zoos have to make milk for a baby bear, they use puppy milk formula because it's most like mother bear's milk. So Cindy mixed puppy milk with half-and-half (half milk and half cream) for extra fat, then added cod-liver oil and vitamins.

That night Cindy took the twins home with her. She didn't sleep at all—she was too busy tube-feeding milk to the cubs, cleaning them, and checking on every little cry. When dawn came, the small bears were still clinging to life.

DIVIDING A MONTH INTO THREE PARTS

To figure out how many times a month Cindy took the bears home with her, we can circle every third day on the calendar below. By counting the circled days, we can see that Cindy took the bears home ten times in a month that is thirty days long.

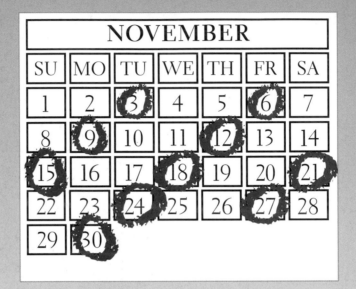

The chart below shows that this month can be divided into three equal parts of ten days each. Each part is equal to $\frac{1}{3}$, or one-third of the month. So Cindy, Denny, and Dr. Kenny each spend $\frac{1}{3}$, or one-third, of the month taking care of the bears at night.

$\frac{1}{3}$	$\frac{1}{3}$	$\frac{1}{3}$
10 DAYS	10 DAYS	10 DAYS
CINDY	DENNY	DR. KENNY

THE CUBS SNUGGLE TOGETHER IN THE INCUBATOR.

At first the cubs needed to eat every two hours, or twelve times a day. Dr. Kenny, Cindy, and Denny (another veterinary technician) took turns bringing them home at night. Every third night, it was Cindy's turn. At five o'clock she put the two bears into a box padded with fleece to keep them warm, packed lots of bottles of milk, and loaded the cubs, their food, and a portable incubator into her car. Once home, she unpacked, made dinner, then fed and cleaned the bears. Snow was no trouble. She drank her bottle and went right back to sleep. But Klondike screamed a lot.

TWELFTHS AND THIRDS

When Klondike and Snow were two weeks old, they each drank twelve bottles of milk in one full day. Since one bear's daily portion of milk—the set—was twelve bottles, each bottle was $\frac{1}{12}$, or one-twelfth, of the set.

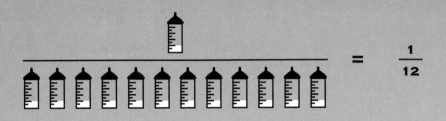

The chart below shows that one-twelfth is a smaller fraction than one-third. When the denominator is a bigger number, the whole amount is divided into more parts, so each part is smaller. You can also see that the fraction four-twelfths, or $\frac{4}{12}$, is equal to one-third, or $\frac{1}{3}$. These two equal fractions are called **equivalent fractions.**

$\frac{1}{12}$	$\frac{1}{12}$	$\frac{1}{12}$	$\frac{1}{12}$	$\frac{1}{12}$	$\frac{1}{12}$	$\frac{1}{12}$	$\frac{1}{12}$	$\frac{1}{12}$	$\frac{1}{12}$	$\frac{1}{12}$	$\frac{1}{12}$
$\frac{1}{3}$				$\frac{1}{3}$				$\frac{1}{3}$			

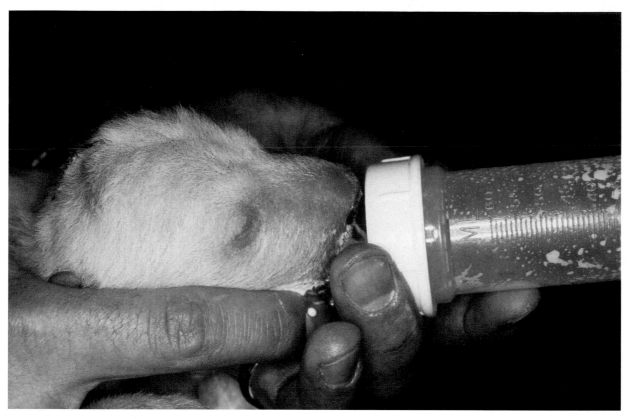

KLONDIKE DRINKS ALL THE MILK IN HIS BOTTLE.

After two weeks, the cubs' weight had doubled. Snow was doing well, but Klondike had a tight, swollen belly. He didn't seem to be digesting the milk he was being fed.

Dr. Kenny ran some tests and consulted with other doctors. They decided not to add cod-liver oil to the milk anymore, but to use safflower oil instead. The doctors also felt that the bears were drinking too much milk.

With a smaller amount of the new milk, Klondike started to feel better. He was still fussy at night, so sometimes Cindy put him in a sleeping bag with her and let him suck on her finger. As the cubs' fur grew thicker, their bodies stayed warm enough outside the incubator. Both of them liked to sleep on Cindy's pillow.

EIGHTHS AND TWELFTHS

By the time Klondike and Snow were one month old, they drank more milk but they were fed less often. In a full day each bear drank eight bottles of milk. For each bear the whole amount, or set, was eight bottles, so one bottle was $\frac{1}{8}$, or one-eighth, of the set.

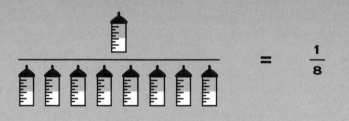

You can see on the chart below that $\frac{1}{12}$, or one-twelfth, is a smaller fraction than $\frac{1}{8}$, or one-eighth.

$\frac{1}{12}$	$\frac{1}{12}$	$\frac{1}{12}$	$\frac{1}{12}$	$\frac{1}{12}$	$\frac{1}{12}$	$\frac{1}{12}$	$\frac{1}{12}$	$\frac{1}{12}$	$\frac{1}{12}$	$\frac{1}{12}$	$\frac{1}{12}$
$\frac{1}{8}$		$\frac{1}{8}$		$\frac{1}{8}$		$\frac{1}{8}$		$\frac{1}{8}$		$\frac{1}{8}$	

"WHO SAYS IT'S BEDTIME?"

18

SHHH! THE CUBS ARE SLEEPING AT LAST!

When the bears were one month old, they slept in a wooden box together. Klondike liked to be near Snow. He pulled himself over to his sister and sucked on her paw. Then he would continue moving around, climbing on top of Snow or burrowing underneath her.

Sometimes Snow acted like she was in pain, crying out between feedings. She didn't like it when Klondike touched her. Cindy began to worry that Snow was too quiet and inactive. Dr. Kenny took X rays of the bears. The X rays showed that both bears had tiny breaks in many of their bones. Klondike and Snow had a disease called rickets.

FRACTIONS OF A 24-HOUR DAY

Klondike and Snow were at the zoo hospital every day from eight in the morning until five o'clock at night. They spent nine hours at the zoo. The next fifteen hours they spent at the home of Cindy, Denny, or Dr. Kenny.

Since there are twenty-four hours in a day, you can see from the chart below that three hours is equal to $\frac{1}{8}$, or one-eighth, of a day. Nine hours is three times that much. It is equal to $\frac{3}{8}$, or three-eighths, of a day. Fifteen hours is equal to $\frac{5}{8}$, or five-eighths, of a day.

$\frac{1}{8}$	$\frac{1}{8}$	$\frac{1}{8}$	$\frac{1}{8}$	$\frac{1}{8}$	$\frac{1}{8}$	$\frac{1}{8}$	$\frac{1}{8}$

HOURS

3   6   9   12   15   18   21   24

$$9 \text{ HOURS} = \frac{3}{8} \text{ DAY} \qquad\qquad 15 \text{ HOURS} = \frac{5}{8} \text{ DAY}$$

So the bears spent three-eighths of every day at the zoo and five-eighths of the day at a caretaker's house.

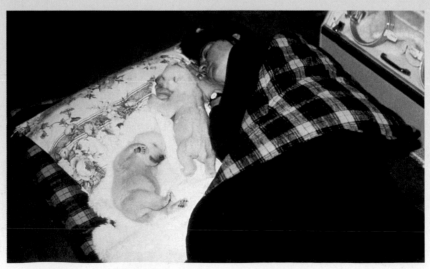

THE CUBS SNOOZE WITH CINDY.

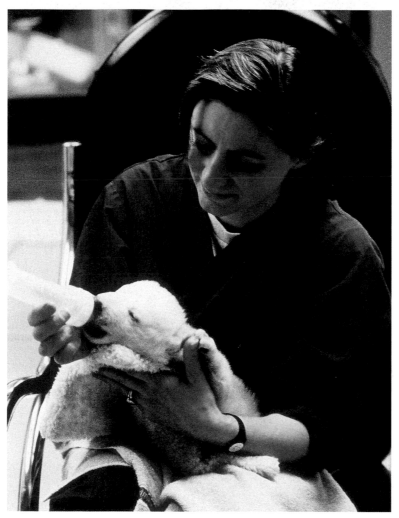

Rickets is caused by a lack of vitamin D, which the body needs in order to absorb calcium and build strong bones. Right away both cubs were given an injection of vitamin D, and their milk was once again made with cod-liver oil, because it has a lot of vitamin D in it. This time the milk didn't bother Klondike's stomach.

Since Snow had been growing faster than Klondike, her bones were more affected by the rickets. The two bears were separated so that Snow could rest without having her brother bumping her or climbing over her. Snow had trouble getting comfortable and often whimpered to be held. Cindy comforted the small bear and hoped the new milk would make her feel better.

MAKING POLAR BEAR MILK USING HALVES

When Klondike and Snow were two months old, the zoo staff decided that the bears needed more protein in their milk to help them grow faster. The original recipe had $\frac{1}{3}$, or one-third, puppy milk.

Because puppy milk has more protein than half-and-half, Cindy knew she had to use a bigger fraction of puppy milk in the recipe.

So she increased the amount of puppy milk in the recipe to $\frac{1}{2}$, or one-half, of the whole amount. The chart below shows that $\frac{1}{2}$, or one-half, is bigger than $\frac{1}{3}$, or one-third.

$\frac{1}{3}$	$\frac{1}{3}$	$\frac{1}{3}$
$\frac{1}{2}$		$\frac{1}{2}$

Cindy mixed 2 cups of puppy milk with 2 cups of half-and-half.

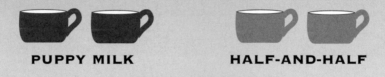

PUPPY MILK   **HALF-AND-HALF**

Since the whole amount was in four equal parts you could say:
   Two parts, or $\frac{2}{4}$, were puppy milk.
   Two parts, or $\frac{2}{4}$, were half-and-half.
But the puppy milk is supposed to be $\frac{1}{2}$, or one-half, of the whole amount, not $\frac{2}{4}$, or two-fourths. The chart below shows that $\frac{1}{2}$ and $\frac{2}{4}$ are equivalent, or equal, fractions.

$\frac{1}{4}$	$\frac{1}{4}$	$\frac{1}{4}$	$\frac{1}{4}$
$\frac{1}{2}$		$\frac{1}{2}$	

After the milk was mixed, cod-liver oil and vitamins were added.

THE CUBS REST ON AN ICE PILLOW.

Both bears got better quickly with cod-liver oil in their milk. A week later, an X ray showed that the cubs' bones had begun to heal. Snow often lay still on the nursery floor like a small bear rug. A physical therapist who had worked with animal patients for a local vet was called in to help Snow strengthen her muscles. Slowly she got stronger.

The cubs started to get their baby teeth, and they fussed because their gums hurt. Cindy soaked towels in water, rolled them up, and put them in the freezer. The bears liked chewing on the frozen towels. Later, Cindy gave them large ice blocks to suck on. Klondike and Snow used the ice as a pillow when they took their naps.

At two months, the bears weighed ten pounds each. But hand-raised polar bears at other zoos had weighed fifteen pounds at two months. Klondike and Snow weren't growing fast enough.

MAKING POLAR BEAR MILK USING FIFTHS

At two and a half months, Klondike and Snow still weren't growing as fast as the zoo staff thought they should be. Cindy needed to change the recipe for bear milk again. She needed to use a formula that had more puppy milk than one-half of the whole amount.

From the chart below, you can see that the fraction $\frac{1}{5}$, or one-fifth, is smaller than $\frac{1}{2}$, or one-half. This goes along with our rule that the bigger the denominator, the smaller the fraction. But when you add three of the one-fifth parts together, you get the fraction $\frac{3}{5}$, or three-fifths, which is bigger than the fraction $\frac{1}{2}$, or one-half.

$\frac{1}{5}$	$\frac{1}{5}$	$\frac{1}{5}$	$\frac{1}{5}$	$\frac{1}{5}$
$\frac{1}{2}$			$\frac{1}{2}$	

Cindy mixed 3 cups of puppy milk with 2 cups of half-and-half to make a whole set of 5 cups.

PUPPY MILK   **HALF-AND-HALF**

Since the whole amount was in five equal parts, you could say:
Three parts, or $\frac{3}{5}$, were puppy milk.
Two parts, or $\frac{2}{5}$, were half-and-half.

1 BATCH OF POLAR BEAR MILK

"GET YOUR PAWS OFF MY BALL!"

The last change to the milk recipe was made at two and a half months, and after that the bears grew rapidly. At three months, Klondike finally weighed a lot more than his sister and could pull himself around on the floor with his front paws. He still had trouble rolling from his back to his stomach. He would paw the air and struggle until he could flip over. Normally a baby bear can walk when he's two months old. Because they had had rickets, Klondike and Snow were late in their development.

With each week that passed, the bears got stronger. One week Klondike was walking around slowly. The next week he could run across the room. Cindy kept working with Snow, helping her stand against a red ball to strengthen her legs. Finally Snow began to walk.

"WHAT DID THEY PUT IN MY MILK?"

At three months, the bears were drinking only four bottles of milk a day (though they also got some milk mixed into their solid food). For each bear the whole amount, or set, was four bottles, so one bottle was $\frac{1}{4}$, or one-fourth, of the whole set.

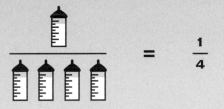 $= \quad \frac{1}{4}$

Instead of drinking eight bottles a day, or one bottle every three hours, as they did when they were one month old, the bears were now drinking four bottles a day, or one every six hours. From the chart below, you can see that $\frac{1}{4}$, or one-fourth, is a bigger fraction than $\frac{1}{8}$, or one-eighth. In fact one-fourth is twice as big as one-eighth. One-fourth and two-eighths are equivalent, or equal, fractions.

$\frac{1}{8}$	$\frac{1}{8}$	$\frac{1}{8}$	$\frac{1}{8}$	$\frac{1}{8}$	$\frac{1}{8}$	$\frac{1}{8}$	$\frac{1}{8}$
$\frac{1}{4}$		$\frac{1}{4}$		$\frac{1}{4}$		$\frac{1}{4}$	

26

When the cubs were about three months old, Cindy began to mix canned dog food with the bears' milk. Klondike liked to turn his bowl over and dump the mixture on the floor. Sometimes Snow would crawl through the spilled milk. Then her brother would lick the food off her fur.

The bears were now old enough to learn to swim. Cindy and Denny set up a swimming pool in the nursery. Klondike got right in the pool, but Snow was cautious. She watched Klondike swim underwater, like a furry submarine. Denny had to pick her up and put her in the pool.

When the bears were five months old, they were big enough to leave the nursery and go to a regular zoo exhibit. At first they were afraid to go in the large outdoor pool. Cindy and Dr. Kenny wore wet suits and swam in the pool, coaxing the bears to join them. Before long, however, the bears grew so big and powerful that it was too dangerous for humans to be with them anymore.

KLONDIKE LOVES PLAYING WITH A PUMPKIN.

Both bears grew a lot in their first year of life. During the next few years, Klondike grew much bigger than Snow. Adult male polar bears are usually much bigger than female polar bears.

When Snow was full-grown, she weighed about 450 pounds, while Klondike weighed about 900 pounds. If you want to compare Snow's weight to Klondike's weight using a fraction, it would look like this:

$$\frac{\text{SNOW'S WEIGHT IN POUNDS}}{\text{KLONDIKE'S WEIGHT IN POUNDS}} = \frac{450}{900}$$

In the chart below, you can see that 450 pounds is $\frac{1}{2}$, or one-half, of 900 pounds.

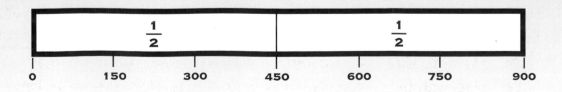

So Snow weighs one half as much as Klondike.

HAPPY BIRTHDAY, KLONDIKE AND SNOW!

Shortly after their first birthday, Klondike and Snow went to SeaWorld in Orlando, Florida. Cindy and Dr. Kenny flew with them on the plane from Colorado to Florida. The bears settled into their new home quickly and were soon catching the trout that swam around in their new pool.

When Cindy went to visit the bears a few years later, she watched them play and wrestle in the water. Klondike and Snow had grown into beautiful, healthy adult animals. After a time, the bears got out of the pool. Klondike went to the back of the exhibit to wait for his dinner, but Snow came toward the glass where the visitors were watching. Suddenly she got very excited, stood on her hind legs, and pounded on the glass with her paws. Even after all the time that had passed, Snow still recognized Cindy.

CINDY HELPS THE BEARS STRENGTHEN THEIR LEGS.

"THERE'S PAPA BEAR!"

SNOW PLAYS PEEKABOO.